Oxford**basics**

SIMPLE SPEAKING ACTIVITIES

Oxford**basics**

Simple Speaking Activities

JILL HADFIELD
CHARLES HADFIELD

OXFORD
UNIVERSITY PRESS

OXFORD

UNIVERSITY PRESS

Great Clarendon Street, Oxford OX2 6DP

Oxford University Press is a department of the University of Oxford.
It furthers the University's objective of excellence in research, scholarship,
and education by publishing worldwide in

Oxford New York

Auckland Cape Town Dar es Salaam Hong Kong Karachi
Kuala Lumpur Madrid Melbourne Mexico City Nairobi
New Delhi Shanghai Taipei Toronto

With offices in

Argentina Austria Brazil Chile Czech Republic France Greece
Guatemala Hungary Italy Japan Poland Portugal Singapore
South Korea Switzerland Thailand Turkey Ukraine Vietnam

OXFORD and OXFORD ENGLISH are registered trade marks of
Oxford University Press in the UK and in certain other countries

First published 1999
2009 2008 2007 2006
10 9

ISBN-13: 978 0 19 442169 0
ISBN-10: 0 19 442169 4

Typeset by Mike Brain Graphic Design Limited, Oxford

Printed in China

ACKNOWLEDGEMENTS
Illustrations by Margaret Welbank

Contents

Foreword

There is a formidable range of materials published worldwide for teachers of English as a Foreign Language. However, many of these materials, especially those published in English-speaking countries, assume that the teachers using them will be working with smallish classes and have abundant resources available to them. Also many, if not most, of these materials make implicit culturally-biased assumptions about the beliefs and values of the teachers and learners.

This situation is ironic in view of the fact that the vast majority of English as a Foreign Language classrooms do not correspond at all to these conditions. Typically, classes are large, resources are limited, and teachers have very few opportunities for training and professional development. Also, the cultural assumptions of teachers and learners in many parts of the world may vary quite significantly from those of materials writers and publishers.

This book is an attempt to address this situation. The authors present 30 lessons at elementary level, each with the same methodological framework. The lessons are explained in clear, accessible language, and none of them require sophisticated resources. Instead, they call on the basic human resources which all teachers and learners bring with them to class. The language points covered are ones found in a typical elementary course, and the topics are those which form part of everybody's daily lives, for example families, homes, and leisure activities.

Most importantly, however, the book offers a framework for teachers who lack training and support. The hope and the expectation is that such teachers will begin by following each step of a lesson quite closely but, as their confidence increases, will adapt and add to the techniques presented here, responding to the particular needs and abilities of their learners.

This is an important book: one of the few attempts to address the problems of the 'silent majority' of teachers worldwide who have little or no training, and few resources to work with.

ALAN MALEY
Assumption University
Bangkok, Thailand

Introduction

English is taught all over the world, by all sorts of teachers to all sorts of learners. Schools and classrooms vary enormously in their wealth and their provision of equipment. Learners are very different from place to place. But, whatever the conditions in which you are working, there is one resource which is universal and unlimited: the human mind and imagination. This is probably the one single most valuable teaching and learning resource we have. Nothing can replace it. In even the most 'hi-tech' environment, a lack of imagination and humanity will make the most up-to-date and sophisticated resources seem dull; conversely, the most simple resources can be the most exciting and useful.

We have been fortunate to spend quite a lot of our time working not only in 'hi-tech' environments with computers and video, but also in classrooms where there is little more than blackboard and chalk and some out-of-date coursebooks. Some of our most interesting learning and teaching experiences (as Confucius said, a teacher is 'always ready to teach; always ready to learn') have been not in the comfortable well-resourced small classrooms of a private language school, but in classrooms where only the minimum of equipment has been available. Equally, some of our most memorable teaching experiences in 'hi-tech' classrooms have been when we have abandoned the cassette or video or glossy coursebook and got to work with that most precious resource of all, the learners' own experience and imagination.

Teachers often have to use materials which are out of date, or contain subject-matter irrelevant to their particular group of learners. For example, we have had great difficulty explaining the concepts of the fridge-freezer and microwave oven to Tibetans. In the same way, learners who have spent all their lives in northern countries might have difficulty with an exercise from an African textbook which asks if they prefer yam or cassava. So over the last few years we have been trying to design materials which can be used in as wide a range of teaching situations as possible.

The activities we suggest are as flexible as the human imagination is creative; they are 'teacher resource material' which teachers will be able to adjust to suit their particular environment. In thinking about universally applicable, 'lo-tech' materials we have come up with a list of criteria that need to be met. The materials will need to:

- be usable in large classes as well as small.
- be suitable for adult learners as well as secondary learners, and if possible easily adaptable to a primary context.
- be centered on the universals of human experience.

- cover the main language skills and have a useful base of grammar and topic vocabulary.
- be traditional enough to be recognizable by all teachers, and thus give them a sense of security, while providing communicative activities for learners.
- be non-threatening in the demands they make on learners.
- be teacher-based 'resource material' rather than books for learners.
- assume that no technical and reprographic resources are available and be based on the human resource rather than the technical.
- be culturally neutral, not context-bound, and thus be flexible, easily adaptable by the teachers to their own culture and teaching context.
- be flexible enough to complement a standard syllabus or coursebook.

Simple Speaking Activities

This book contains thirty activities, designed according to the criteria above, for developing the speaking skill at elementary level. Each activity has three main stages:

- **Setting up**—This introduces the learners to the topic. The activity may be demonstrated to the whole class, or learners may make materials to be used during the speaking practice.
- **Speaking practice**—This is the main part of the activity. The learners communicate with each other in pairs or groups, or compete as teams.
- **Feedback**—The learners come back together as a whole class. A few of them may report to the rest of the class on things they have talked about in their pairs or groups. This is the time when the teacher gives feedback on the language practised, and deals with any problems.

Setting up

It is especially important in speaking activities, when learners are often working in pairs or small groups, that they know exactly what to do. If they are confused, much valuable speaking time will be wasted and no-one will enjoy the lesson. Many of the activities in this book start with a demonstration of things the learners will do later in their pairs or groups. A demonstration can be done:

- On your own in front of the class as, for example, in 16 'Rooms in a flat' and 25 'Jobs'.
- With a learner, or learners, in front of the class as, for example, in 3 'Numbers' and 14 'Describing people'.
- With the whole class as, for example, in 2 'The alphabet' and 7 'Nationalities'.

However clear you think the demonstration has been, it is always a good idea to double check that everyone knows what to do.

Other activities begin with the learners preparing materials that they will use later on. For example in 5 'Personal information' the learners copy a form that they will later fill in with their partner's details, and in 29 'Describing actions 1' they prepare pieces of paper with actions written on them that they will later share.

The setting-up stage of the lesson is also a good time to practise the pronunciation of any words and phrases that you know your learners will find difficult. You will find help with many common problems in the 'Pronunciation points' section of each lesson.

Speaking practice

A speaking lesson is a kind of bridge for learners between the classroom and the world outside.

speaking practice

learning new language using language to
in the classroom communicate in real life

In order to build this bridge, speaking activities must have three features. They must give the learners *practice opportunities* for *purposeful communication* in *meaningful situations*.

Compare these two activities:

Activity 1

TEACHER	*'You must do your homework.' Repeat.*
LEARNERS	*'You must do your homework.'*
TEACHER	*Good. 'You must arrive at eight o'clock.' Ben?*
BEN	*'You must arrive at eight o'clock.'*
TEACHER	*Good. 'Listen to the teacher.' Sara?*
SARA	*'You must listen to the teacher.'*

Activity 2

Setting up

1 Tell the learners that you would like them to think of good rules for learning English. Write one or two examples on the board:

You must speak English in class.

You mustn't speak [mother tongue] in class.

Give them a few minutes to think on their own.

3

Discussion

2 Put the learners in groups of three or four and ask them to share their ideas. Remind them to use 'must' and 'mustn't'.

3 Tell them to prepare Ten Rules for Learning English and to write them down on a sheet of paper.

4 When all the groups have finished making their rules, collect their ideas and write them up on the board.

The most obvious difference between the two activities is in the way they are organized. In Activity 1 the teacher is talking, first to the whole class, then to individual learners. In Activity 2 the learners are talking to each other in small groups.

This type of learner–learner interaction in pairs or groups provides far more practice in using the language than the more traditional teacher–learner interaction. In a class of twenty learners, a twenty-minute activity where the teacher asks the learners questions will give the learners a total of only about ten minutes' speaking time, i.e. half a minute each. And the teacher (who doesn't need the practice!) gets ten whole minutes' speaking time. In contrast, a twenty-minute activity where learners are working in groups, asking and answering each other's questions, will give them many more opportunities for practice.

Both activities provide a lot of repetition of the structure 'must (+ verb)', and both do so in a fairly controlled way. In Activity 1, the control is provided by the teacher who tells the learners what to do. In Activity 2, control is provided by the example sentences on the board. However, Activity 1 provides repetition with no context. The sentences are random and unrelated. Such repetition is virtually meaningless: the learners are simply repeating the structure. They have no idea why they are saying the sentences, and in fact it would be possible to do the activity without understanding a word! In Activity 2, there is a context—making rules for learning English—and all the communication is related to this context. This makes the activity much more meaningful for the learners.

In Activity 1, the learners have no sense of purpose in producing their sentences; they are merely doing what the teacher tells them, and the only purpose of their repetition is to practise the structure. In Activity 2, however, the learners have a goal—making the rules—and the language is used for the purpose of achieving this goal. This mirrors real-life situations much more closely, as well as making the activity more interesting and motivating for the learners.

There are many different techniques which can be used to create meaningful contexts for speaking practice in English. For example:

- **Ask and answer**—Learners ask and answer questions.
- **Describe and draw**—Learners work in pairs. Learner A has a picture which learner B cannot see. Learner A describes the picture and learner B draws it.
- **Discussion**—Learners work in pairs or groups to find out each other's ideas or opinions on a topic.
- **Guessing**—The teacher, or some of the learners, have information which the others have to guess by asking questions.
- **Remembering**—Learners close their eyes and try to remember, for example, items from a picture or the location of objects in the classroom.
- **Miming**—A learner mimes, for example, a feeling or action which the others have to identify.
- **Ordering**—Learners arrange themselves in a particular order (for example, alphabetical) by asking questions until they find their correct position.
- **Completing a form/questionnaire**—Learners ask and answer questions, or provide information, in order to complete a form or questionnaire.
- **Role play**—Learners act out an imaginary situation. The learners either use a dialogue, or the teacher gives them instructions about what to say.

There are examples of all these techniques in this book.

Materials

Several of the activities in this book need no materials at all. Where materials are needed, they are usually very easy to prepare. For example, some activities require every learner to have a small piece of paper or card with information on it: 4 'Telling the time' and 7 'Nationalities' are two of these. The information is always very brief, so they will not take long to prepare. Indeed, in some cases, for example 12 'Shapes' and 30 'Describing actions 2', the learners make the pieces of paper themselves as part of the activity.

In several of the activities, we have provided pictures, plans, or questionnaires for you to copy. These may be drawn on the board, on large pieces of paper ('posters'), or on pieces of card ('flashcards'). In the case of large pictures and plans, posters have obvious advantages over drawings on the board: you can prepare them in advance and they can be stored and used again. Try to find a cheap source of large sheets of paper for posters. In Madagascar, for example, the teachers we worked with found the sheets of paper used for wrapping vegetables in the market were ideal for making posters. A good way to fix posters or flashcards to the board is to pin a length of string along the top of the board like a clothes-line. You can then use clothes-pegs to peg your posters to the string!

Some activities need two different posters, one at the back and one at the front of the class. Learners then sit in pairs, one facing the front and one facing the back. The reason for this is to create an 'information gap'. Each learner has different information which they have to exchange. The posters can be pictorial, for example the two comic figures in 13 'Parts of the body', or written, for example the two half-dialogues in 23 'Leisure activities'.

Real objects or 'realia' can be used as an alternative to drawings, for example in 21 'Shopping'.

Classroom organization

If your learners are new to working in pairs and groups, you will need to introduce these ways of working with care. Here are some tips to help you:

- Introduce pair- and groupwork gradually. First get your class used to doing very simple activities, practising language they are confident with. At first the activities should not be too long—for example you could introduce a short one at the end of a lesson.
- Tell the learners who to work with rather than giving a vague instruction like 'Find a partner' or 'Get into groups of four'. If your class is working in pairs and you have an odd number of learners, make one a group of three.
- It is important to give clear signals to show when each stage of the activity begins and ends. For example, when you want learners to begin an activity you should say 'Start now' or 'Go', and when you want them to stop, you should clap your hands, ring a bell, or—perhaps most effective—silently raise your hand. You can teach them to raise their hands too as they stop talking. This way the silence spreads like a ripple.

The teacher's role

While learners are working together in pairs or groups, you have the opportunity to give them individual attention. There are several roles you might need to adopt:

- *Explainer*—If some learners have not understood what to do or have problems with the language, you will need to help them. If a large number of learners have the same problem, it is probably better to stop the activity, explain to everyone, and then start again.

■ *Controller*—If the activity gets too noisy, you will have to quieten things down. (You could use the technique just mentioned of raising your hand and getting the learners to raise theirs.) You will also have to make sure as far as you can that all the learners are speaking English. This means you will have to be quick on your feet!

■ *Evaluator*—These activities give you a valuable opportunity to listen to your learners and evaluate their progress, both as individuals and as a whole class. You can get a lot of feedback from listening to them to help you decide whether they have understood and you can move on, or whether they need more teaching. You can also give them feedback on their problems. It is best not to interrupt the activity as this can impede fluency and undermine their confidence. Carry a piece of paper with you, note down errors and problems, and deal with them in the feedback stage.

Feedback

When the activity is over, it is important to bring the class back together again. If the activity has involved, for example, a discussion or a questionnaire, ask a few learners to report back to you and the rest of the class, for example:

TEACHER *Maria, now, you and Helen. What can you both do?*
MARIA *We can both sing. We can both play … check …*
TEACHER *Chess?*
MARIA *We can both play chess.*

It is also important to give feedback on the language practised. Use the notes you made while monitoring the activity as the basis of your feedback. In the case of grammar and vocabulary errors, try writing them on the board and ask the learners if they can see what is wrong. If a large number of learners have made the same mistake, you might need to spend some time explaining or clarifying it. Make sure they have understood and perhaps ask them to do the activity again with a different partner. You might also like to make this language problem the topic of another lesson at a later date. This is also a good stage in the lesson to focus on persistent pronunciation problems.

Pronunciation points

Each activity contains suggestions for pronunciation work. The pronunciation points dealt with arise directly out of the language being presented in the activity. While it is impossible to address every problem that users of the book will encounter, we have made an attempt to cover points that many learners will find troublesome, like stress patterns, intonation in different types of question and statement, and some work on individual sounds, focusing on those that give trouble most often such as long and short vowels, or the /θ/ sound. Suggestions for teaching the learners to produce individual sounds are given in each activity. In general, a useful technique is to get the learners to produce and practise the sound in isolation first, then go on to produce it in a word, and then to produce the word in a sentence.

Stress

There are various techniques for practising stress patterns, both in individual words and in sentences, for example:

- Get the learners to clap out the rhythm before saying the word or sentence.
- Get the learners to tap out the rhythm on their desks as they repeat the sentence.
- Dictate the word or sentence and get the learners to mark the stress.

Intonation

The main patterns dealt with are:

- Falling intonation in question-word questions, for example:

  Where's the station?

- Rising intonation in yes/no questions, for example:

  Do you like fish?

- Falling intonation in answers and negative statements, for example:

  No, there isn't any sugar.

- Falling intonation in commands, for example:

  You mustn't smoke.

There are various techniques for practising intonation patterns, for example:

- Show with hand movements how the voice rises or falls.
- Get the learners to make appropriate hand movements up or down as they repeat the sentences.
- Get the learners to mirror the rise or fall physically, for example when they repeat a yes/no question get them to begin the question in a seated position and to stand up as their voice rises at the end of the sentence.

■ Dictate the sentence and get the learners to mark the intonation arrows up or down.

Building a lesson

There are two companion books to this one, *Presenting New Language* and *Simple Listening Activities*. Each of these also contains thirty activities, and in all three books the topics and the language presented and practised correspond. So, for example, activity 1 in all three books is about 'Greetings and introductions' and activity 30 is about 'Describing actions'. The activities in each book are graded, following a basic structural syllabus. This means that you can design your own lesson or sequence of lessons using material from one, two, or all three books, depending on your learners' needs and the time available.

Activities

1 Greetings and introductions

LANGUAGE	Hello. My name's _____.
	What's your name?
	Nice to meet you.
TECHNIQUE	Role play.
MATERIALS	The dialogue below.
PREPARATION	None.
TIME GUIDE	20 minutes.

Setting up

1 Divide the class into two groups of equal size. Get the groups to form two circles, one inside the other. The learners should face each other in pairs, like this.

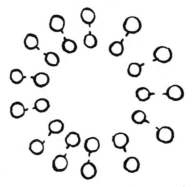

The learners in the outer circle are 'A's and those in the inner circle are 'B's.

2 Tell the pairs to introduce themselves to each other like this:

LEARNER A   Hello. My name's _____. What's your name?
LEARNER B   My name's _____. Nice to meet you.
LEARNER A   Nice to meet you too.

Role play

3 Get everyone in the outer circle (the 'A's) to move a step to the right, so that they are facing a new partner. This time, the 'B's in the inner circle should start the dialogue:

LEARNER B   Hello. My name's _____, etc.

4 Get the 'A's in the outer circle to continue moving round until they have gone all the way round and are back where they started. 'A's and 'B's should take turns in starting the dialogue.

Feedback

5 Review any common pronunciation problems the learners had.

12

Pronunciation points
- Practise the stress patterns in the dialogue:

  Hello. My name's Ben. What's your name?

  My name's Kate. Nice to meet you.

  Nice to meet you too.

- Practise falling intonation in question-word questions:

  What's your name?

Comment

This is a good activity to use at the beginning of a course or school year when, especially if the class is large, they may not know one another well. This activity, as well as needing a lot of space, can get quite noisy, so if you can, do it outside.

2 The alphabet

LANGUAGE   The letters of the alphabet.

TECHNIQUE   Completing a grid.

MATERIALS   A list of the letters of the alphabet in random order.

PREPARATION   Make the list of letters.

TIME GUIDE   30 minutes.

Setting up

1   Tell the learners to draw a grid like this:

2   Tell the learners to work alone and choose fifteen letters from the alphabet—they can be any letters they like. They should write one letter in each square of their grid.

3   Tell the learners that you are going to call out a list of letters in random order. When they hear you call out a letter that is in their grid, they should cross it out. The first learner to cross out all their letters is the winner.

Completing a grid

4   Divide the learners into groups of three or four. One person in each group should write down the letters of the alphabet in random order, as you did. The other members of the group should draw new grids and fill them with letters.

5   The learners can then take turns in playing the game in their groups.

Feedback

6   Review any problems the learners had in pronouncing the letters of the alphabet.

The letters of the alphabet divide into seven sound groups. The phonemes for the sound groups are as follows:

A H J K	/eɪ/
B C D E G P T V	/iː/
F L M N S X Z	/e/
I Y	/aɪ/
O	/əʊ/
Q U W	/uː/
R	/aː/

Comment

This activity is based on a game called 'Bingo' which is popular in Britain. This is usually played with numbers rather than letters. When someone has crossed out all the numbers on their grid, they call out 'Bingo!'

3 Numbers

LANGUAGE	Numbers.
	What's your number? **It's _____.**
TECHNIQUE	Ordering.
MATERIALS	Cards with the numbers you want to teach on them. There should be one card for each learner in your class.
PREPARATION	Make the cards.
TIME GUIDE	20 minutes.

Setting up

1 Ask for five volunteers to come to the front of the class. Give each learner a card with a number from one to five.

2 Write the following speech bubbles on the board:

3 Tell the volunteers to find out each other's numbers using the dialogue on the board. They should then arrange themselves in the order of the numbers on their cards.

Ordering

4 Collect the cards from the volunteers, add them to your other cards, and mix them up.

5 Give each learner in the class a card and ask them all to stand up. Tell everyone to arrange themselves in a line from the smallest number to the largest. Show them where the person with the smallest number should start the line. Remind them that they must use the dialogue and not show their cards to anyone else.

Feedback

6 Review any sequences of numbers the learners had problems with.

Pronunciation point ■ Practise /θ/ in 'three'. Teach the learners to make this sound by putting their tongue between their teeth and breathing out.

Comment If you want to practise a limited sequence of numbers, for example 1 to 10, use several sets of cards and divide the learners into groups. This activity, as well as needing a lot of space, can get quite noisy so, if you can, do it outside.

4 Telling the time

LANGUAGE   **What time is it?**
It's _____ o'clock.

TECHNIQUE   Ordering.

MATERIALS   Pieces of paper with a time of day written on them in figures (for example 12.15, 3.45, 5.30)—there should be one for each learner in your class; small pieces of card to make clock faces (see below).

PREPARATION   Prepare the pieces of paper and card.

TIME GUIDE   20 minutes.

Setting up

1 Divide the class into groups with about ten learners in each group. Tell each group to find a space and mark a 'clock face' on the floor with pieces of card, like this:

2 Give each learner a piece of paper with a time written on it. Tell them not to show it to other members of their group.

Ordering

3 Tell them to arrange themselves round the clock face according to the times written on their pieces of paper. They should do this by standing where they think the hour hand on the clock should be.

4 They should then ask the other learners standing near them the time.

> What time is it?
> It's _____ o'clock.

If necessary, they should change their position. When they have finished, they might be standing round the clock face like this:

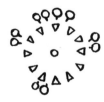

(The times this group of learners had were: 12.00, 12.15, 2.30, 2.45, 6.45, 7.00, 9.30, 10.00, 11.15, 11.45.)

5 Collect the pieces of paper and redistribute them. This time, you could turn the activity into a race—but make sure there is no cheating and learners do not look at each other's pieces of paper!

Feedback

6 Review any times the learners had problems with.

Pronunciation points

- 'O'clock' is pronounced /əklɒk/.
- Practise falling intonation in question-word questions:

What time is it?

5 Personal information

LANGUAGE	What's your name/address?
	How do you spell that?
	How old are you?
	Where are you from?
	My name's _____.
	I'm _____.
	I'm from _____.
	Numbers, alphabet.
TECHNIQUE	Completing a form; guessing.
MATERIALS	The form below, on the board.
PREPARATION	None.
TIME GUIDE	30 minutes.

Setting up

1   Draw this form on the board and tell the learners to copy it:

NAME ....

AGE ....

ADDRESS ....

....

PLACE OF BIRTH ....

2   Ask for a volunteer to come to the front. Ask him or her the following questions:

What's your name?
How do you spell that?
How old are you?
What's your address?
Where are you from?

Fill in the form on the board as the learner replies.

Completing a form

3   Ask two learners to come to the front. Get one to ask the questions and fill in the form for the other. (Put the questions up in speech bubbles on the board if you think they need this support.)

4   Tell the class to work in pairs, asking and answering the questions and filling in their own copies of the form for each other.

Guessing

5   Collect in the forms. Pick one at random from the pile. Tell the class whether the person described in the form is a 'he' or a 'she'. Get them to identify the person described by asking:

How old is he/she?
What's his/her address?
Where is he/she from?

Feedback

6   Ask some learners what they found out about their partners, for example:

TEACHER *Mark, how old is John?*
MARK   *He's ... elv—.*
TEACHER *... eleven ...*
MARK   *He's eleven.*
TEACHER *Good. And where's he from?*

Pronunciation points

▪   Practise /h/ in 'how'. Teach the learners to make this sound by pretending to laugh (Ha! Ha!) while holding a sheet of paper in front of their mouths. The paper should move.

▪   Practise falling intonation in question-word questions:

What's your name?

How do you spell that?

6 Countries

LANGUAGE   'Countries' vocabulary area (for example, **France**, **Italy**, **Argentina**).

Where is ___?
It's in _____.
Which country is/are _____/s from?
He's/she's/it's from _____.
They're from _____.

TECHNIQUE   Ask and answer.

MATERIALS   Pieces of paper for all the learners.

PREPARATION   Think of six cities, six kinds of food, and six famous people your
learners are likely to know.

TIME GUIDE   30 minutes.

Setting up

1 Put questions like these on the board:

Where is   Paris?

                Rome?

                Buenos Aires?, etc.

Which country   is   spaghetti   from?

                 are   curry

                          hamburgers, etc.

Which country   is   [6 names of famous people]   from?

2 Give all the learners pieces of paper and tell them to tear them into
six smaller pieces. Then divide the class into groups of three. The
first member of each group should write one of the cities on each
of his or her pieces of paper, the second member should do the
same with the 'food' words, and the third with the famous people.

Ask and answer

3 Tell the groups to put all their pieces of paper face down in a pile
on a desk in the middle of the group. Tell them to mix them up.

4 Tell them to take it in turns to pick up a piece of paper and ask the
appropriate question to the other two learners in the group. The
first to answer the question correctly should be given the piece of
paper. The learner with most pieces of paper at the end is the
winner.

Feedback

5 Check the answers with the class.

Pronunciation points

■ Make sure the learners know where the stress falls in the names of countries, for example:

•
America

•
Argentina

•
Italy

Comments

If the learners are confident, rub the questions off the board after they have written the words on their pieces of paper. However, leave them up if you think they need help.

The countries shown here are examples. If you feel other countries are of more interest to your learners, substitute them for the examples given.

7 Nationalities

LANGUAGE	'Nationalities' vocabulary area (for example, **English**, **Chinese**, **Brazilian**). **Are you _____?** **Yes, I am.** **No, I'm not.**
TECHNIQUE	Guessing.
MATERIALS	2 identical sets of about 10 pieces of paper with a nationality written on each (or one set for each group if you do this activity in small groups).
PREPARATION	Prepare the pieces of paper.
TIME GUIDE	20 minutes.

Setting up

1 Tell the class to imagine that you come from a different country. Tell them you are going to draw pictures on the board and they should try to guess what nationality you are. Here are some ideas:

2 Begin drawing and get them to ask questions while you draw, for example:

Are you French?
Are you Australian?

Guessing

3 Rub out your drawings and draw a line down the middle of the board. Divide the class into two teams of equal size. Put the two sets of pieces of paper face down on your desk.

4 Ask one learner from each team to come to the board and give them a piece of chalk each. Get them to take a piece of paper from the top of their pile.

5 Tell them to draw pictures on the board, as you did. The other members of their team should try to guess what nationality they are, asking 'Are you _____?'

6 When a team has guessed correctly, the next member of that team should come to the board, take a piece of paper, and draw. The team that finishes first is the winner.

Feedback

7 Review any nationalities the learners seemed unsure about.

Variation

You can do this activity in small groups, if you prefer. Give each group some sheets of paper to draw on, and a set of pieces of paper with nationalities written on them. Tell them to put the pieces of paper face down in the centre of their group.

In turn, each learner should take a piece of paper and draw a picture representing the nationality written on it. The rest of the group should try to guess the nationality.

Pronunciation points

- Practise /ə/ (not /æ/) in 'African', 'Australian', 'Indian', 'Italian'.
- Sometimes the stress falls on the same syllable in country and nationality words, for example:

Africa, African

America, American

… and sometimes on a different syllable, for example:

Egypt, Egyptian

Italy, Italian

- Practise rising intonation in yes/no questions:

Is she Greek?

Are they Australian?

8 Locating objects

LANGUAGE	'Everyday objects' (for example, **bag**, **flowers**, **book**) and 'classroom furniture' (for example, **table**, **windowsill**, **desk**) vocabulary areas.
	Where's the/my _____? **Where are the/my _____?**
	Place prepositions (for example **on**, **in front of**, **behind**).
TECHNIQUE	Remembering.
MATERIALS	None.
PREPARATION	None.
TIME GUIDE	30 minutes.

Setting up

1   Close your eyes, then ask the class to tell you where something is, for example:

TEACHER   *Where's my bag?*
LEARNERS   *It's under the table.*

2   With your eyes still closed, get learners to ask you where one or two things in the classroom are, for example:

LEARNER   *Where are the flowers?*
TEACHER   *They're on the windowsill.*

Remembering

3   Tell the learners each to prepare eight questions about the location of objects in the classroom. Put speech bubbles on the board if you feel they need support:

> Where's the _____?
>   my

> Where are the _____?
>   my

> It's   on   the _____.
> They're in front of
>   behind

4   Then get them to work in pairs. One in each pair should close his or her eyes and the other should ask the questions he or she has prepared. The learner with closed eyes should try to reply from memory.

5   Then the other learner should ask his or her questions.

Feedback

6   Revise any prepositions the learners had problems with by asking individual learners about the location of objects in the classroom.

Pronunciation points

▪   Practise the stress patterns in the replies to the questions:

It's under the table.

They're on the windowsill.

9 Feelings

LANGUAGE   'Feelings' vocabulary area (for example, **tired**, **happy**, **hungry**).

Are you _____?
Yes, I am.
No, I'm not.

TECHNIQUE   Miming.

MATERIALS   2 identical sets of about 10 pieces of paper with a 'feeling' word written on each.

PREPARATION   Prepare the pieces of paper.

TIME GUIDE   30 minutes.

Setting up

1   Draw a speech bubble on the board:

       Are you _____?

2   Mime a feeling to the class, for example 'tired' by yawning or 'happy' by smiling. Get the learners to ask you how you feel, for example 'Are you tired?' Reply 'Yes, I am' or 'No, I'm not' as appropriate.

3   Choose a confident learner and give him or her one of the pieces of paper with a 'feeling' word written on it. Tell the learner to mime the adjective and get the rest of the class to guess what the feeling is.

Miming

4   Divide the class into two teams of equal size. Put the two sets of pieces of paper face down on your desk.

5   Get a member of each team to come to the front of the class and take a piece of paper from their team's pile. They should mime the feeling written on it until someone in their team guesses correctly.

6   Then another member of the team should come to the front, take the next piece of paper from the pile, and mime the feeling written on it for the rest of the team to guess, and so on.

7   The first team to finish the pieces of paper wins.

Feedback   **8** Review any pronunciation problems the learners had.

Pronunciation points   ◼ Many learners confuse /æ/ as in 'angry' and /ʌ/ as in 'hungry'.
Teach them the difference between these sounds. Get them to make
/æ/ first with their mouths open. Then get them to round their lips
and put their tongues back for /ʌ/. Make sure they put the /h/
sound at the beginning of hungry (but not at the beginning of
angry!)

◼ Practise rising intonation in yes/no questions:

⟶

Are you tired?

⟶

Is she hungry?

Comment   This activity can also be adapted for pairs or small groups.

10 Families

LANGUAGE	'Families' vocabulary area (for example, **father, mother, sister**).
	Who's this?
	This is my _____.
	He/she's _____ years old.
	Is this your _____?
	Yes, it is.
	No, it isn't.
TECHNIQUE	Ask and answer.
MATERIALS	Sheets of paper for all the learners.
PREPARATION	None.
TIME GUIDE	40 minutes.

Setting up

1 Give all the learners sheets of paper.

2 Ask them to close their eyes and imagine a photograph of their whole family. Give them a little time to do this, then ask them to draw their 'photo' on their sheet of paper.

Ask and answer

3 Ask for a volunteer to come to the front and copy his or her photo on the board. Ask him or her to describe the people in the picture, for example 'This is my father. He's 47 years old.' Help the learner by asking questions, for example 'Who's this?', 'Is this your mother?'

4 Then get the learners to work in pairs telling each other about the people in the photos they have drawn. Put model questions and answers in speech bubbles on the board to help them, for example:

Who's this?

This is my _____.

Is this your _____?

Yes, it is.

No, it isn't.

Feedback   Ask a few learners to describe their photo to the rest of the class.

Pronunciation points

■ Practise /θ/ in 'father', 'mother', 'brother'. Teach the learners to make this sound by putting their tongue between their teeth and breathing out.

■ Practise the stress patterns in the following sentences:

This is my sister.

She's six years old.

11 Colours

LANGUAGE   'Colours' (for example, **blue**, **red**, **brown**) and 'everyday objects' (for example, **plate**, **pencil**, **envelope**) vocabulary areas.

Have you got a _____ _____?
Yes, I have.
No, I haven't.

TECHNIQUE   Ask and answer.

MATERIALS   Sheets of paper for all the learners; coloured pencils.

PREPARATION   None.

TIME GUIDE   40 minutes.

Setting up

1   Give all the learners sheets of paper. Tell them to tear them into six pieces.

2   Get them to draw one everyday object on each piece, for example a plate, a pencil, an envelope. Demonstrate one or two simple drawings on the board, for example:

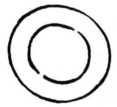 

3   Tell the learners to colour each of the objects, or label them with the name of a colour if they do not have coloured pencils. Each object should be a different colour. They should also write a list of their objects on a separate piece of paper, for example:

a blue pencil

a red hat

a yellow book

a brown envelope

a green cup

a white plate

Ask and answer

4   Put the learners into small groups of three or four. Ask them to put their drawings together face down and mix them up. Then each person in the group should take six drawings.

32

5 Tell the learners that they must get their own pictures back by asking questions. If necessary, write a model dialogue in speech bubbles on the board as support, for example:

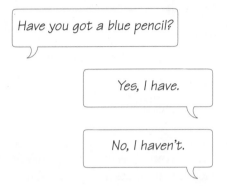

Have you got a blue pencil?

Yes, I have.

No, I haven't.

The learners should take turns asking questions, like this:

LEARNER 1 TO LEARNER 2   *Have you got a red plate?*
LEARNER 2   *Yes, I have.* [gives learner 1 picture of red plate]
LEARNER 2 TO LEARNER 3   *Have you got a brown envelope?*
LEARNER 3   *No, I haven't.*
LEARNER 3 TO LEARNER 1   *Have you got a green book?*

6 When they get a picture back, they should cross that item off their lists.

Feedback

7 Practise pronunciation by holding up some of the learners' pictures and getting the whole class to repeat the description of the object, for example, 'a yellow book', 'a green cup'.

Pronunciation points

■ Some learners have problems with /l/ in 'blue', 'yellow', and 'black', and /r/ in 'green', 'grey', and 'brown'. Teach them to make the /l/ sound by putting the tip of their tongues on the part of the mouth just behind the upper teeth and pulling it away quickly as they make the sound. For the /r/ sound their tongues should curl back and not press against the top of the mouth.

33

12 Shapes

LANGUAGE   'Shapes' vocabulary area (for example, **thin**, **round**, **square**).

Have you got anything _____?
Yes, we have. We've got a _____ _____.
No, we haven't.

TECHNIQUE   Ask and answer.

MATERIALS   Sheets of paper for all the learners.

PREPARATION   None.

TIME GUIDE   40 minutes.

Setting up

1   Divide your class into groups of about five learners and give each learner a sheet of paper. Tell the groups that they must draw objects of a certain shape, for example:

Group 1   thin objects

Group 2   round objects

Group 3   square objects

Group 4   triangular objects

Ask and answer

2   Collect all the drawings of shapes and mix them together. Redistribute them so each group has drawings of objects of a variety of shapes. Make sure the groups know the names of the objects.

3   Tell each group to hide their drawings from the rest of the class.

4   Tell the groups that they must now get back their own drawings. They must do this by asking the other groups for them. For example tell a learner from group 1 to ask the other groups, in turn, 'Have you got anything thin?' The other groups should reply, for example, 'Yes, we have. We've got a thin pencil' or 'No, we haven't' as appropriate. If they have got a drawing of something thin, they should give it to group 1.

Feedback

5   If possible, display the drawings in their 'shape' groups. Ask the learners if they can think of the names of more objects of each shape.

Pronunciation points

- Practise the /θ/ sound in 'thin' and 'thick'. Teach the learners to make this sound by putting their tongues between their teeth and breathing out.
- Practise the short /ɪ/ sound in 'thin' and 'thick'. (Some learners may substitute a long /iː/ sound.) Show how the /ɪ/ sound is much shorter than /iː/, and there is no 'smiling' movement of the lips.
- Practise the stress pattern in:

  Have you got anything round?

13 Parts of the body

LANGUAGE	'Parts of the body' (for example, **arm**, **foot**, **hand**) and 'colours' (for example, **blue**, **brown**, **black**) vocabulary areas.

He/she's got a _____ _____.
He/she's got _____ _____/s.
His/her _____/s is/are _____.

TECHNIQUE	Describe and draw.
MATERIALS	Two posters of comic figures with contrasting features; sheets of paper for all the learners.
PREPARATION	Make the posters.
TIME GUIDE	30 minutes.

Setting up   **1**   Divide the learners into pairs. Ask one learner in each pair to turn round so they are facing the back of the room. The other should stay facing the front. Put one poster up at each end of the room, for example:

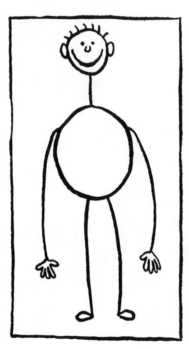

Describe and draw   **2**   Tell the learners facing the front of the room to describe the poster they can see to their partner (who is facing the other way). Their partner should draw it on his or her sheet of paper. No peeping! If necessary, put up a poster of model sentences in speech bubbles as support, for example:

36

He/she's got a _____ _____.

He/she's got _____ _____/s.

His/her _____/s is/are _____.

3 Get the learners facing the back of the room to describe their poster in the same way. This time the learners facing the front of the room should draw.

4 Tell the learners facing the back to turn round. Take down the poster at the back of the room and put it up beside the other one. Get the learners to make sentences comparing their drawings, for example 'He's got big feet; he's got small feet.'

Feedback

5 Draw a third comic figure on the board with different features to the ones on the two posters. Ask learners to describe it, if necessary using the speech bubbles.

Pronunciation points

■ Practise the stress patterns in:

He's got big feet.

His arms are short.

14 Describing people

LANGUAGE 'Describing people' (for example, **tall, thin, young**), 'parts of the body' (for example **hair, eyes, nose**), and 'colours' (for example, **blue, brown, black**) vocabulary areas.

We are both _____.
We have both got _____ _____/s.

TECHNIQUE Discussion.

MATERIALS None.

PREPARATION None.

TIME GUIDE 30 minutes.

Setting up

1   Ask a learner who has some things in common with you to come to the front of the class. Pre-teach 'both' by standing beside him or her, gesturing, and talking about the things you have in common, for example:

   We are both tall.
   We have both got dark hair.

2   Write the following speech bubbles on the board:

   We are both _____.

   We have both got _____ _____/s.

3   Ask for two volunteers to come to the front of the class and say what they have in common. Tell them to use the language in the speech bubbles.

Discussion

4   Get the learners to work in pairs. Tell them to make notes about the things they have in common. Give a time limit of five minutes.

5   Ask pairs to stand up and tell the rest of the class the things they have in common, using the language in the speech bubbles.

Feedback

Ask a few learners to make new sentences using 'We are both' and 'We have both got' about themselves and other learners in the class.

Pronunciation points

■ Practise /ʃ/ in 'short'. Teach the learners to make this sound by first making the /s/ sound (as in 'sort') and then moving the tongue back and curling up the edges to make /ʃ/.

■ Practise /θ/ in 'thin'. Teach the learners to make this sound by putting their tongues between their teeth and breathing out.

15 Clothes

LANGUAGE	'Clothes' (for example, **skirt**, **blouse**, **T-shirt**) and 'colours' (for example, **blue**, **white**, **yellow**) vocabulary areas.
	He/she's wearing a _____ / _____s.
TECHNIQUE	Remembering.
MATERIALS	None.
PREPARATION	None.
TIME GUIDE	30 minutes.

Setting up

1 Give each row of learners alternate letters, A and B, so that the learners are divided into columns of As and Bs like this:

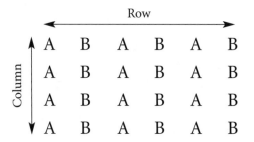

2 Tell each column of As and Bs to turn and study the column of learners opposite them. They should try to remember exactly what they are wearing. Give them two minutes to memorize the details.

Remembering

3 Group the learners in pairs so that As are working with the Bs opposite them.

4 Tell all the Bs to close their eyes. Tell the As to describe all the other learners in the B column to their partner. The Bs should try and name each description, for example:

LEARNER IN COLUMN A *She's wearing a blue skirt and a white blouse.*
LEARNER IN COLUMN B *Anna?*
LEARNER IN COLUMN A *No. Anna's wearing a white T-shirt.*
LEARNER IN COLUMN B *Oh … yes … it's Sara!*

5 Then all the As should close their eyes. Tell the Bs to describe all the other learners in the A column to their partner. This time the As should try and name each description.

Feedback

6 Ask individual learners to describe the person they remember most vividly.

Variation

At stage 4, tell all the Bs to close their eyes. Tell the As to make some changes in their appearance, for example taking off a watch or exchanging sweatshirts. Then tell the Bs to open their eyes and say what changes they can see, for example:

LEARNER B *Peter's wearing a blue jacket now … and Helen isn't wearing a watch.*

Pronunciation points

- Practise the /ɜː/ sound in 'shirt', 'skirt', 'T-shirt'. In British English the 'r' is not pronounced in these words.
- Practise the /aʊ/ sound in 'blouse' and 'trousers'. Teach the learners to make this sound by rounding their lips, and then slowly closing their mouths.

Comment

This activity is set up for the traditional classroom with rows of desks facing the front. If your classroom is arranged in a different way, get your learners to work in groups who are sitting near one another. Each group should contain five or six learners.

16 Rooms in a flat

LANGUAGE   'Rooms' vocabulary area (for example, **living-room**, **kitchen**, **bedroom**).

This is the _____.
Here's the _____.
The _____ is next to/opposite the _____.

TECHNIQUE   Discussion.

MATERIALS   Plan of a flat, on a poster or on the board; sheets of paper for all the learners.

PREPARATION   Make the poster, if you are using one.

TIME GUIDE   30 minutes.

Setting up

1   Put up a plan of your ideal flat, or draw one on the board. For example, if you like cooking, include a big kitchen and if you like reading, include a library. Tell the learners about it, for example:

> This is a flat I would like to live in. There's a big kitchen. That's good because I love cooking. I like reading too, and this little room here is my library—where I keep my books. … etc.

Discussion

2   Get the learners to draw a plan of their ideal flat or house.

3   When they have finished, tell them to work in pairs. They should show their partner the plan they have drawn and tell them about it. Write the following phrases on the board to help them:

There is   _____ _____/s.
     are

This is the _____.

Here's the _____.

The _____ is next to   the _____.
             opposite

| Feedback | 4 | Ask a few learners to tell the rest of the class about their partners' houses. Review any common pronunciation problems the learners had. |

Variation

Tell the learners to work in pairs. If possible, get them to sit back to back. Give them a few minutes to think about these two questions:

What kind of person is their partner?
What kind of flat or house would their partner like?

Then ask them to draw the plan of a flat or house they think their partner would like. When they have finished, tell the pairs to show each other their plans and describe all the rooms.

Pronunciation points

■ Practise /ɪ/ in 'is', 'kitchen', 'living-room'. Many learners make this sound too long, like /iː/ in 'leave'. One way of emphasizing the contrast between short and long sounds is to put your hands wide apart, as if stretching a piece of elastic, for long sounds, and then bring them close together for short sounds.

17 Furniture

LANGUAGE   'Furniture' vocabulary area (for example, **sofa**, **armchair**, **table**).
           Place prepositions (for example, **near**, **beside**, **between**).

TECHNIQUE Discussion.

MATERIALS Plan of a living-room, on a poster or on the board; sheets of paper
           for all the learners.

PREPARATION Make the poster, if you are using one.

TIME GUIDE 40 minutes.

Setting up

1   Put up a plan of a living-room, or draw one on the board, for
    example:

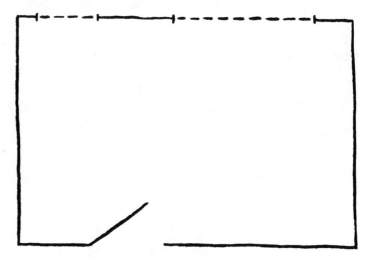

Beside the plan write a list of furniture with prices, for example:

sofa	£400
armchair	£200
table	£150
television	£200
rug	£50
picture	£100
cupboard	£200

Choose items that the learners are likely to have in their homes.

2   Tell the learners to copy the plan.

Discussion

3 Tell the learners that they each have £1,000 to spend on new living-room furniture. Tell them to decide what to buy from the list on the board and where to put it in their living-room. They should draw it in on their plan.

4 When they have finished drawing in their furniture, tell them to get into pairs. They should tell their partner what they bought and where they put it.

Feedback

5 Ask a few learners to tell the rest of the class about their partners' living-rooms. Review any common pronunciation problems the learners had.

Variation

You could do a more elaborate version of this activity with a plan of a whole flat or house. Obviously the list of furniture would be longer, and the amount of money would have to be larger!

Pronunciation points

■ Practise /tʃ/ in 'armchair' and 'picture'. Teach the learners to make this sound by placing the tips of their tongues on the part of the mouth just behind the upper teeth (as if they were going to make a /ʃ/), and then releasing it to make a /tʃ/.

■ Practise /əʊ/ in 'sofa' and /eɪ/ in 'table', showing how each of these sounds combine two different vowels.

Comment

We have used British pounds in the example, but this activity will probably be more interesting for your learners if you use your own currency.

18 In town

LANGUAGE	'Town' vocabulary area (for example, **market**, **park**, **baker**).
	Is there a _____? **Yes, there is.** **No, there isn't.** **Where's the _____?**
	Place prepositions (for example, **next to**, **opposite**, **near**).
TECHNIQUE	Describe and draw.
MATERIALS	Simple plan of an imaginary town, on a poster or on the board; two sheets of paper for all the learners.
PREPARATION	Make the poster, if you are using one.
TIME GUIDE	40 minutes.

Setting up

1 Put up the poster, or draw the town plan below on the board.

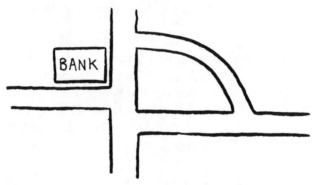

Tell the learners to make two copies each.

2 While the learners are making their copies, write up a list of places on the board, for example:

market	bank
park	post office
baker	cinema
butcher	cafe
supermarket	disco

Describe and draw

3 Tell the learners, still working on their own, to take one of their copies and design a town. They can choose places from the list and put them anywhere on the plan. Tell them they can leave places out if they like (for example, no supermarkets), or have more than one of something (for example, five discos).

4 Divide the learners into pairs, A and B. Tell them to keep the towns they have designed well hidden from their partners!

5 Tell all the As to take their blank plans and the Bs to take the towns they have designed. The As should ask the Bs questions about where places are in their towns and draw them onto their blank plans, for example:

LEARNER A *Is there a cinema?*
LEARNER B *Yes, there is. It's next to the cafe.*
LEARNER A *Where's the cafe?*
LEARNER B *It's opposite the market.*

6 When the As have finished their copies of the Bs' town designs, tell the Bs to ask the As questions in the same way.

7 When both the As and the Bs have finished, tell the learners to compare their copies with the originals. Are they accurate?

Feedback

8 Ask a few learners questions about their town designs. Review any common pronunciation problems the learners had.

Pronunciation points

■ Contrast the short vowel /æ/ in 'bank', 'cafe', and the long vowel /ɑː/ in 'market', 'park'. For the /æ/ sound, the mouth is open and lips pulled back as if smiling. For the /ɑː/ sound, the lips are further forward and rounded to make the longer sound, and the tongue goes down and back.

■ Practise falling intonation in question-word questions:

Where's the bank?

■ and the stress patterns of the answers:

It's next to the post office.

It's opposite the cinema.

It's behind the market.

19 Directions

LANGUAGE 'Town' vocabulary area (for example, **church**, **market**, **cinema**).

How do I get to the _____?
Go straight on.
Turn right.
Turn left.

Imperatives.

TECHNIQUE Role play.

MATERIALS Simple plan of your town centre, on a poster or on the board.

PREPARATION Make the poster, if you are using one.

TIME GUIDE 30 minutes.

Setting up

1 Put up the poster, or draw a simple plan of your town centre on the board. Here is an example:

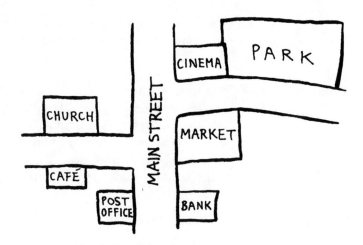

2 Write a list of the most important places in the centre on the board, for example:

church/mosque

market

cinema

bank

park

Role play

3 Ask the learners to imagine they are standing outside, for example, the post office. Pretend you are lost and ask them how to get to the first place on the list, for example:

TEACHER *Excuse me, I'm a stranger here. Can you help me? How do I get to the church?*

LEARNER *Go down Main Street … turn left. The church is on your right, opposite the cafe.*

4 Repeat the procedure with the next place on the list.

5 Divide the learners into pairs and tell them to take turns in directing each other to the other places on the list.

Feedback

6 Review any common pronunciation problems the learners had.

Variation

Use a plan of your school instead of one of your town centre. Ask learners to imagine they are at the main entrance. Ask them how to get to various rooms, for example the Head Teacher's office, their classroom, the gym.

Pronunciation points

■ Practise the consonant cluster /str/ in 'street' and 'straight'. Get the learners to build up the cluster one consonant at a time, for example 'reet–treet–street' and 'raight–traight–straight'.

■ Practise falling intonation in commands and instructions, for example:

Go straight on.

Turn left.

20 In the market

LANGUAGE 'Food' vocabulary area (for example, **apples**, **rice**, **fish**).

Is there any _____?
Are there any _____?
Yes, there is some _____.
Yes, there are some _____.
No, there isn't any _____.
No, there aren't any _____.

TECHNIQUE Remembering.

MATERIALS Poster of a market.

PREPARATION Make a poster by copying the picture below onto a large piece of paper. If necessary, change the kinds of food in the picture to the foods available in your country.

TIME GUIDE 30 minutes.

Setting up

1 Tell the learners that you are going to show them a picture of a market, but only for a few seconds. They must concentrate very hard and try and remember what is for sale in the market.

2 Hold the poster up in front of the class, but only briefly.

Put it down again. Ask the learners what they can remember, for example:

TEACHER *Can you remember what there is? Ben, are there any apples?*
BEN *Yes, there are some apples.*
TEACHER *Good. Now is there any rice? Maria?*
MARIA *Yes, there is a ... some rice.*

Remembering

3 Divide the learners into pairs. Hold up the picture again for a few seconds. Put it down and tell the learners, in their pairs, to discuss what they can remember.

If you feel it is necessary, write some phrases on the board to help them:

Is   there any _____?
Are

Yes, there is   some _____.
                 are

No, there isn't any   _____.
            aren't

4 Ask some of the pairs what they can remember.

Feedback

Hold up the poster again. How good were the learners' memories? Review any common pronunciation problems the learners had.

Pronunciation points

■ Practise falling intonation in negative statements:

No, there isn't any sugar.

No, there aren't any apples.

21 Shopping

LANGUAGE	'Containers' and 'food and drink' vocabulary areas (for example, a bag of flour, a bottle of lemonade, a tin of soup). Have you got any _____? Yes, I have. How much/many would you like? I'd like one/two, etc. bags/tins, etc., please. Sorry, no I haven't.
TECHNIQUE	Ask and answer.
MATERIALS	About 10 different kinds of food and drink in containers, or a poster listing different kinds of food and drink with pictures of each; sheets of paper for all the learners.
PREPARATION	Make the poster, if you are using one. If you are using real food and drink, arrange the items at the front of the class where all the learners can see them.
TIME GUIDE	40 minutes.

Setting up

1   Place about ten items of food and drink on a table at the front of the class, or put up the poster. Point to each item, checking learners know the vocabulary and pronunciation.

2   Tell the learners to choose five items, and write them down in a list on their sheets of paper. They should give different amounts for each of the items they choose, for example:

> two tins of soup
>
> a kilo of apples

Ask and answer

3   Ask half the learners to stand up and tell the other half to remain in their seats. The first half are the 'shoppers' and the others are the 'shopkeepers'. The lists the shoppers have made are their shopping lists. The lists the shopkeepers have made are the items they have in their shops.

4 Tell the shoppers to go round the shops, finding the items on their lists. If you feel it is necessary, write some phrases on the board to help them:

Have you got any _____?

Yes, I have. How many would you like?

Sorry, no I haven't.

I'd like	*one*	*bag/s,*	*please.*
	two	*tin/s*	
		bottle/s	

When a shopper finds a shopkeeper who has an item he or she wants, both learners should tick that item on their lists. When the shoppers have found all the items on their lists, they should sit down.

5 When the 'shoppers' have sat down, tell them to become 'shopkeepers'. All the 'shopkeepers' should stand up and become 'shoppers'. The learners should repeat the activity in their new roles.

Feedback

Write any common mistakes the learners made on the board and see if they can recognize, and correct, them.

Variation

You can make this activity a competition if you like by setting a time limit—say five minutes. The shopper who has 'bought' the most items in that time is the winner.

Pronunciation points

■ Practise the stress patterns in:

I'd like two tins please.

■ Practise rising intonation in yes/no questions:

Have you got any soup?

22 Food and drink

LANGUAGE 'Food and drink' vocabulary area (for example, **bananas, hamburgers, tea**).

Do you like _____?
Very much; quite; not very much; not at all.

TECHNIQUE Completing a questionnaire.

MATERIALS Sheets of paper for all the learners.

PREPARATION For the questionnaire, choose six to ten different kinds of food that your learners know.

TIME GUIDE 40 minutes.

Setting up

1 Write a questionnaire grid like this on the board (use kinds of food and drink that your learners know).

Do you like ...

	very much	quite	not very much	not at all
bananas				
hamburgers				
chocolate				
yoghurt				
tea				
orange juice				

2 Check that the learners know the difference between 'very much', 'quite', 'not very much', and 'not at all'.

3 Ask for a volunteer to come to the front of the class. Ask him or her the question: 'Do you like bananas?' He or she should reply 'Very much', 'Quite', 'Not very much', or 'Not at all'. Tick the appropriate box. Continue with the other items of food and drink.

Completing a questionnaire	**4**	Rub out the first learner's replies and ask for two more volunteers to come to the front. Get one of them to ask the other the questions, and to tick the appropriate boxes.

5 Rub out the replies again. Give the learners sheets of paper and ask them to copy the questionnaire.

6 Divide the learners into pairs. Tell them to put their partner's name at the top of their copy of the questionnaire. Then they should ask their partners the questions and tick the appropriate boxes.

Feedback

7 Ask individual learners to report back to the whole class on their partners' likes and dislikes. Write sentence frames up on the board to help them:

_____ likes _____ very much.

He/she quite likes _____.

He/she doesn't like _____ very much.

He/she doesn't like _____ at all.

Pronunciation point

■ Practise /ə/ in words like 'banana', 'hamburger' and 'yoghurt'. This vowel sound is very common in unstressed syllables in English.

23 Leisure activities

LANGUAGE   'Leisure activities' vocabulary area.

Do you like _____?
Yes, I love it.
Not very much.
No, I hate it.

TECHNIQUE   Role play.

MATERIALS   'Half-dialogue' posters (see below).

PREPARATION Make the posters.

TIME GUIDE 30 minutes.

Setting up   1   Divide the class into pairs like this:

A – B   A – B   A – B

A – B   A – B   A – B

A – B   A – B   A – B

A – B   A – B   A – B

A – B   A – B   A – B

Tell the Bs to turn round and face the back of the class. The As
should remain facing the front. Put up half-dialogue A at the front
of the room and half-dialogue B at the back.

Half-dialogue A	*Half-dialogue B*
A: Do you like swimming?	A:
B:	B: Not very much—and it's too cold today.
A: Do you like cycling then?	A:
B:	B: It's OK, but I haven't got a bicycle. Do you like table tennis?
A: No, I hate it!	A:
A:	B: Well, do you like going to the cinema then?
A: Yes, I love it!	A:
B:	B: Good. So do I!

56

2 Tell the learners that it's Saturday afternoon and, in their pairs, they are deciding what to do. Read the complete dialogue with them, telling the As to repeat part A and the Bs to repeat part B after you.

Role play

3 Get the whole class to read the dialogue in chorus, with all the As taking the role of A and all the Bs taking the role of B.

4 Then get them to practise the dialogue in their pairs.

5 Take down the half-dialogues and replace them with these role-play posters:

Role-play A

It's Saturday afternoon. You want to do something with your friend. Ask them what they like doing.

Role-play B

It's Saturday afternoon. You want to do something with your friend. Ask them what they like doing.

Get the learners to decide what to do together. Tell them they can use sentences from the dialogue they practised in the first part of the lesson.

Feedback

6 Ask some of the pairs to tell the rest of the class what they decided to do. Review any common pronunciation problems the learners had.

Pronunciation points

- Practise /ɪŋ/ in 'swimming' and 'cycling'. Teach the learners to make this sound through their noses.
- 'Do you like', when spoken quickly, is pronounced /dʒəlaɪk/.
- Practise the stress patterns in:

  Not very much.

  Yes, I love it.

  No, I hate it.

24 Daily routines

LANGUAGE	'Everyday actions' vocabulary area (for example, **get up**, **have breakfast**, **go to work**).
	When do you _____? **First, last.**
	Telling the time.
TECHNIQUE	Completing a questionnaire.
MATERIALS	A set of flashcards or board drawings of verbs showing daily routines: get up, have breakfast/lunch/dinner, go to work, go home, go to bed; sheets of paper for all the learners.
PREPARATION	Make the flashcards, or copy the drawings below on the board.
TIME GUIDE	40 minutes.

Setting up

1 Make a 'picture substitution table' using these pictures, either as flashcards stuck to the board, or as board drawings:

When do you   [get up]   ?

I   *[have breakfast]   at _____ o'clock.*

                [go to work]

                [have lunch]

                [go home]

                [have supper]

                [watch TV]

                [go to bed]

2 Ask individual learners questions from the table, for example:

TEACHER *Helen, when do you get up?*
HELEN *I get up six.*
TEACHER *You get up at six. That's early!*

Completing a questionnaire

3 Write a questionnaire grid like this on the board (use the verbs in the substitution table).

When do you …

	me	friend 1	friend 2	friend 3
get up				
have breakfast				
go to school/work				
have lunch				
go home				
have supper				
watch TV				
go to bed				

5 Tell the learners to copy the questionnaire grid on their sheets of paper. Tell them to fill in the first ('me') column.

6 Divide the class into groups of three or four. Tell the learners, working in their groups, to take turns asking the other members of the group what time they get up, have breakfast, etc. They should fill in the details on their questionnaire grids.

Feedback

7 Ask the groups questions about the information they have collected, for example:

In your group, who gets up first?

Who goes home last?

Pronunciation points

■ Practise short vowel sounds:

/e/ in 'bed', 'get', 'breakfast'.

/ʌ/ in 'up', 'lunch'.

25 Jobs

LANGUAGE 'Jobs' vocabulary area (for example, **factory worker**, **postman**, **farmer**).

Simple present tense.

TECHNIQUE Miming.

MATERIALS Two (or more) sets of ten pieces of paper with the names of jobs written on them.

PREPARATION Prepare the pieces of paper; practise the mimes.

TIME GUIDE 30 minutes.

Setting up

1 Divide the class into two teams, A and B (if your class is very large, have a C and a D team as well).

2 For each team, have ready a set of ten pieces of paper with the name of a job written on each one. For example:

factory worker	*postman*
farmer	*teacher*
businessman/ woman	*secretary*
doctor	*bus driver*
farmer	*hairdresser*

Put the sets in piles on your table at the front of the class. The sides with the writing on should be face down.

3 Take a piece of paper from one of the sets and mime the job that is on it. Invite the class to guess what job it is. When they have guessed, return the piece of paper to the bottom of the set.

Miming

4 Explain that each team has their own set of pieces of paper. Get one learner from each team to come to the front and take a piece of paper from the top of their set. He or she should return to the team and mime the job written on it. The team must guess what the job is.

5 When a team has guessed a job, get the next learner from that team to come up and take a piece of paper. The first team to finish miming and guessing all the jobs are the winners.

Feedback

6 Revise any names of jobs the learners had difficulty with.

Variation

Instead of guessing the job from a mime, get the teams to guess by asking questions, for example:

Does this person work indoors?
Does this person wear a uniform?
Does this person work in an office?

Pronunciation points

- Practise the /ə/ sound at the end of many 'jobs' words, for example: 'worker', 'farmer', 'teacher', 'doctor' (in British English the 'r' is not pronounced).
- Note that '-man' at the end of words like 'postman' and 'businessman' is pronounced /mən/, not /mæn/.

26 Housework

LANGUAGE	'Housework' (for example, **make the beds, sweep the floor, do the shopping**) and 'families' (for example, **mother, father, sister**) vocabulary areas.
	Present simple tense.
	Adverbs of frequency (for example, **always, usually, often**).
TECHNIQUE	Completing a questionnaire.
MATERIALS	None.
PREPARATION	None.
TIME GUIDE	40 minutes.

Setting up

1 Write this questionnaire grid on the board:

In your house, who ...

	me	mother	father	sister	brother
makes the beds					
sweeps the floor					
does the shopping					
washes the dishes					
cleans the windows					

2 Ask a learner the first question. Encourage the learner to use an adverb of frequency, for example:

TEACHER *Sara, in your house, who makes the beds?*
SARA *My mother.*
TEACHER *Does she always make the beds?*
SARA *Yes, always.*

Ask the rest of the questions, filling in the boxes with the learner's answers.

Completing a questionnaire

3 Rub out the answers, and ask a learner to come to the front. He or she should choose another learner in the class and ask the questions and fill in the boxes as you did.

4 Give out sheets of paper to all the learners and tell them to copy the questionnaire grid.

5 Tell them to work in pairs, asking each other the questions and filling in their questionnaire with information about their partner.

Feedback

6 Ask the learners questions about their partners, for example:

TEACHER *Sam, who washes the dishes in Maria's house?*
SAM *Maria's sister.*

Pronunciation points

■ 'Often' is usually pronounced /ɒfn/.
■ Practise the /ʃ/ sound in 'shopping' and 'wash'. Get the learners to make the /s/ sound. Then get them to put their tongues up and back a little to make /ʃ/.

27 Abilities

LANGUAGE | 'Abilities' vocabulary area (for example, **ride a bicycle**, **type**, **play the trumpet**).

We can _____.
We can't _____.
Can you _____?
Yes, I can _____.
So can I.
No, I can't _____.
Neither can I.

TECHNIQUE | Discussion.

MATERIALS | None.

PREPARATION | None.

TIME GUIDE | 30 minutes.

Setting up

1 Draw a line down the middle of the board. On one side write 'We can …' and on the other side write 'We can't …'.

2 Think of three or four common things you can do. Examples might be 'swim', 'ride a bicycle', and 'type'.

3 Ask a learner to come to the front of the class and ask him or her questions, for example:

Can you swim?
Can you type?

When he or she answers 'Yes, I can', say 'So can I' and write the ability on the 'We can …' side of the board.

4 Now think of three or four things you can't do. Examples might be 'play the trumpet', 'run 15 kilometres', and 'ride a camel'.

5 Ask the learner questions in the same way as you did before. When he or she answers 'No, I can't', say 'Neither can I' and write the ability on the 'We can't' side of the board.

6 Tell the class 'We can _____ and _____ . We can't _____ and _____.'

Discussion	**7** Rub the 'abilities' words off the board. Tell the learners to get into pairs. Each pair should make a copy of the two headings on the board. Tell the pairs to find out:

things they can both do
things neither of them can do

8 Put these speech bubbles on the board to help them:

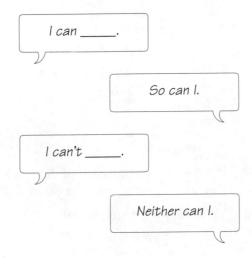

I can _____.

So can I.

I can't _____.

Neither can I.

Feedback	**9** Ask some of the pairs to report back to the class on things they can or can't do.

Variation	If you like, you can make this into a competition. At stage 7, set a time limit of five or ten minutes. The pair with the most things they can and can't do wins.

Pronunciation points	■ Contrast the pronunciation of the vowel in 'can' where it is /æ/, and 'can't' where, in British English, it is /ɑː/.
	■ Practise the stress patterns in phrases like:

Can you ride a bicycle?

Yes, I can.

No, I can't.

So can I.

Neither can I.

28 Rules: 'must' and 'mustn't'

LANGUAGE	**Must, mustn't.**
TECHNIQUE	Discussion.
MATERIALS	Sheets of paper for the groups.
PREPARATION	None.
TIME GUIDE	30 minutes.

Setting up

1 Tell the learners that you would like them to think of good rules for learning English. Write one or two examples on the board:

You must speak English in class.

You mustn't speak [mother tongue] in class.

Give them a few minutes to think on their own.

Discussion

2 Put the learners in groups of three or four and ask them to share their ideas. Remind them to use 'must' and 'mustn't'.

3 Tell them to prepare Ten Rules for Learning English and to write them down on a sheet of paper.

Feedback

4 When all the groups have finished making their rules, ask them for their best ideas and write them on the board.

5 Get the class to vote for the ten best rules. You could make these into a poster for the classroom wall.

Variation

You could ask the learners to make other sets of rules, for example:

school rules
library rules
rules for teachers
rules for bosses

Pronunciation points

- 'Must' is usually pronounced /məst/. It is only pronounced /mʌst/ when it is stressed. 'Mustn't' is always pronounced /mʌsnt/ (note, the first 't' is not pronounced).
- Practise falling intonation in commands, for example:

You must listen carefully.

You mustn't smoke.

29 Describing actions 1

LANGUAGE | 'Leisure activities' (for example, **swimming**, **sewing**, **riding a bicycle**) and 'everyday actions' (for example, **washing**, **eating**, **sleeping**) vocabulary areas.

Are you _____ing?
Yes, I am. No, I'm not.

TECHNIQUE | Miming.

MATERIALS | Sheets of paper for the groups.

PREPARATION | Prepare one or two simple mimes of actions.

TIME GUIDE | 30 minutes.

Setting up

1 Mime an action. Prompt the class to ask: 'Are you _____ing?' Answer 'Yes, I am' or 'No, I'm not'.

2 Put the learners in groups of three or four and give each group a sheet of paper. Tell them to tear it into six pieces. Then ask them to think of some more actions and to write one on each piece.

3 Collect all the pieces of paper from the groups, mix them up, and put them in a pile face down on your desk.

Miming

4 Divide the class into two teams, A and B. Tell one learner from each team to come to the front and take a piece of paper from the pile. He or she should return to the team and mime the action written on it. The team must guess what the action is.

5 When a team has guessed an action, get the next learner from that team to come up and take a piece of paper. The activity ends when all the pieces of paper have been taken. The team with the most pieces of paper are the winners.

Feedback

6 Revise any action words the learners had difficulty in guessing.

Variation

You can also do this activity in small groups. Follow stages 1 and 2 in setting up, but instead of keeping all the pieces of paper yourself, redistribute them so that each group gets a new set. Get each group to put their pieces of paper face down in a pile. One learner in each group should take the first piece and mime the action to the others. The learner who guesses the action correctly takes the next piece of paper.

Pronunciation points   ■   Practise the stress patterns in questions and answers like:

      •
Are you reading?

• •
Yes, I am.

•   •
No, I'm not.

30 Describing actions 2

LANGUAGE	'Everyday actions' vocabulary area (for example, **walk**, **drink**, **play**). Present continuous tense.
TECHNIQUE	Describe and draw.
MATERIALS	Two sheets of paper for each learner.
PREPARATION	None.
TIME GUIDE	50 minutes.

Setting up

1   Draw a window on the board, for example:

2   Give the learners two sheets of paper each and tell them to make two copies of the window. Tell them that it faces out onto a busy street.

3   Write a substitution table like this one on the board:

Two men	is	walking down the street.
A woman	are	drinking milk.
A girl		playing football.
A baby		waiting for a bus.
Two boys		climbing a tree.
A dog		sleeping in the sun.
A cat		eating an ice cream.

4 Ask the learners, working on their own, to make five sentences from the table to describe things they can see through their window.

5 Then tell them to illustrate their five sentences by drawing what they can see on their first copy of the window, for example:

Describe and draw

6 Divide the learners into pairs, A and B. Tell the pairs to hide their drawings from each other. Tell the As to describe their drawings to the Bs. The Bs should listen to the As' descriptions and draw the scene on their second copy of the window. When they have finished, get the pairs to compare their drawings.

7 Then tell the Bs to describe their drawings to the As, and the As to listen and draw. Again, get the pairs to compare their drawings.

Feedback

8 Ask a few learners to describe their drawings to the rest of the class.

Pronunciation points

■ Practise the /ŋ/ sound in 'walking', 'selling', standing', etc. Teach the learners to make this sound through their noses.